METABOOS AND DONE WORKOUTS

100 Metabolic workout to Burn Fat, BUILD MUSCLE WITH LITTLE TIME AND NO EQUIPMENT

Charlie Shirk

CW01670155

COPYRIGHT © 2025 | SUMMER BODY INT. PUBLISHERS
Paperback ISBN: 978-1-965849-30-9
Hardcover ISBN: 978-1-965849-31-6
Printed in The U.S.A

All rights reserved. No part of this program may be reproduced (by any means) without the expressed written consent To The Author.

Disclaimer

The information presented within this book is no way intended as medical advice or to serve as a substitute for medical counselling. The information presented herein should be used in conjunction with the guidance of your physician. Always consult your physician before starting this program as you would with any exercise or nutritional program. If you choose to abstain seeking the consent of your physician throughout this program, you are agreeing to accept full responsibility for your actions.

This information is being provided for educational and informational purposes only.

Please be sure to consult your physician before starting this or any program. There is an inherent risk with physical activity.
The Author cannot be held responsible for any injury that may occur during participation with this program.

Get Your Summer Body With The 75 HARD Challenge

START NOW

"
IF YOU WANT
TO BE A
CHAMPION
YOU NEED
TO TRAIN
LIKE ONE.
-GSP

Table of Contents

THE WORLD OF METABOOST WORKOUTS

Revolutionize Your Fitness: METABOOST ONE AND DONE WORKOUTS 100 Metabolic Workouts to Burn Fat, Build Muscle, and Transform Your Body—All in 20 Minutes or Less!

Are you ready to finally achieve your dream body while staying inspired and motivated along the way? Welcome to *METABOOST ONE AND DONE WORKOUTS*, the ultimate fitness guide that combines powerful metabolic workouts with motivational and inspirational messages to keep you on track.
This book, inspired by Meredith Shirk's groundbreaking fitness methods, is not just about burning fat and building muscle—it's about transforming your entire approach to health and fitness. Whether you're short on time, equipment, or energy, this book delivers results and empowers you to stay consistent and energized.

What Makes METABOOST ONE AND DONE WORKOUTS Unique?

This isn't just another workout book—it's a comprehensive guide to transforming your body and mind. Each chapter includes motivational and inspirational messages to remind you why you started, keep you focused, and help you push through challenges.

Every workout is built around **Excess Post-Exercise Oxygen Consumption (EPOC)**, a proven method to keep your metabolism running high long after you've finished exercising. These quick yet powerful workouts burn calories, sculpt muscles, and keep you energized—all in just 20 minutes a day, without equipment.

What You'll Find in This Book

•**100 High-Impact Workouts:** Transform your body with efficient, no-equipment routines that fit into your busiest days.
•**Motivational Messages:** Each section features uplifting words to boost your morale, helping you stay committed and focused on your goals.
•**Science-Backed Training:** Leverage metabolic training techniques to maximize fat burn, build lean muscle, and improve cardiovascular fitness.
•**Beginner to Advanced Progressions:** Tailored options to meet you at your fitness level, with room to grow.

Why Choose METABOOST?

1.**Maximized Fat Burn:** Each workout is designed to elevate your EPOC, ensuring you burn calories long after you finish.
2.**Efficient and Effective:** Get the results of a long gym session in just 20 minutes of focused effort.
3.**Holistic Transformation:** This book isn't just about your body—it's about building the mindset and habits that lead to long-term success.
4.**Stay Inspired:** With motivational messages throughout, you'll feel encouraged and empowered to stay consistent, even on tough days.

This Book is Your Path to a New You
You deserve a fitness routine that fits your life, inspires your spirit, and delivers real results. With *METABOOST ONE AND DONE WORKOUTS*, you'll discover:
•How to achieve your dream body in less time than you thought possible.
•Workouts that transform your metabolism into a fat-burning machine.
•Uplifting messages to keep you motivated and on track, no matter where you're starting from.

Take Control of Your Fitness Journey Today

Your dream body is within reach, and *METABOOST ONE AND DONE WORKOUTS* is here to guide you every step of the way. Whether you're a busy professional, a parent on the go, or someone looking for a fresh start, this book provides everything you need to succeed.

Benefits of This Kind of Training

8 reasons you need to do these workouts regardless of whether you are a seasoned athlete or just looking to get fitter.

1

Get Results Quickly

This short, intense style of training wakes up your metabolism. This in turn will increase your cardio levels, build lean muscle and burn fat.

2

Higher Levels of Athleticism

Performing even the most basic of exercises with high levels of intensity in a circuit will effectively raise your heart rate and increase your over all levels of athleticism.

3

Lean Muscle Gains

Your body is an amazing machine, when you push its limits, it will respond as needed. In this case that means more HGH (human growth hormones) to keep up with the work load and power outputs.

4

The Mental Push

Mental toughness is a huge aspect in achieving the things you want. Exercise is no different. You must push yourself as hard mentally as you do physically to complete the workouts. If you are an athlete performing these routines as finishers to your main workout, this mental toughness you develop will carry over into your sport, forcing you to work as hard as you can till the end.

5

A Break from the Norm

Exercise at the end of the day should be fun and something you enjoy. Plodding along on the treadmill or road is not fun, it's tedious and frankly quite boring. This kind of training is interesting, challenging and never the same twice. It may be tough while you are doing it, but it's an enjoyable tough.

6

Calorie Burn

It's possible to burn anywhere from 300-650 calories per workout based on your height, weight, gender, fitness levels and intensity. Not bad for something that is less than 30 minutes!

7

The EPOC

I mentioned earlier the benefits of EPOC. The workout in this book are short and intense in nature, setting you up nicely for the EPOC afterburn. The benefits of EPOC have been shown in cases to continue burning calories up to 36 hours after completing the routine. If that isn't enough incentive to put in 100% effort I don't know what is.

The Challenge

These workouts are hard. They will feel like torture when you are grinding through them. You have to constantly remind yourself of the benefits and just how little time the workouts take.

Challenge yourself, beat your former performance and in no time you will look, feel and perform exactly like you want to.

Who is this Book for?

This book is a guideline for anyone who wants to lose weight, get fitter and become overall more athletic. It's for those who are short on time, those who work full time with a family and have no time for the gym. It's for full time moms with kids who get very little time to exercise. It's for full time students who have no cash for a gym membership.

It's also for those who want to push their conditioning levels to new limits. The exercises contained within this book have all been used by me and the fighters I train. After any practise is over, the group with perform one of the circuits listed. When the circuits provided are performed at the end of workouts or practice, they are designed to make sure you have burnt every single bit of energy you have left. They become an exercise in not only conditioning but also mental toughness and satisfaction.

So, if you are looking to drop a little weight, don't have the time or cash for a gym membership or you are a competing athlete looking to push your conditioning levels there is something in this book for you.

"
If It Doesn't
CHALLENGE You
It Doesn't
CHANGE You.
-Zig Ziglar

How to get the Most out of the Workouts

1

-Check in with your physician first. This is the case with any new program and this one is no exception.

2

-Always make sure you know the correct form on any exercise. Form is not only key to getting the most out of any exercise, but it is the way to prevent injuries. Consult a professional who can coach you in the correct form.

3

-Never go into a workout hurt. Training with an injury is just going to slow down your healing and potentially make things worse. Feeling tight or working through DOMS is perfectly fine however.

4

-Be sure to scale the exercises to your level of fitness. Going too heavy too soon is going to hurt you. Be realistic, make proper progressions and you will be a beast in no time.

5

-Be constantly aware of signs of overtraining. Rest is as much a part of training as going hard is. If you are feeling super beat up, stressed, struggling to sleep, fatigued, you need a rest.
Make sure you are always eating well and healthy, resting well, sleeping well and practising stretching and soft tissue work.

6

-Progress at a clever rate. Don't assume you can go from beginner to beast in 1 week. Training strength and conditioning takes time, just like learning a new technique. Consistency and small gains are key.

7

-If you follow this program 100% and put in your maximum effort, you will burn fat and increase fitness levels.

8

-Performing a warm-up is a must. Never underestimate a quality warm-up.

Workout Guidelines

FREQUENCY: HOW MANY DAYS A WEEK DO YOU NEED TO TRAIN?

This is really up to you as an individual. In a perfect world 4 times a week would be ideal. This isn't always an option though. Even just twice a week will make a huge difference to your health, attitude and appearance. As I mentioned earlier if you are training in a sport or martial art, fitting one workout in at the end of practice will be incredibly beneficial to your performance. Depending on your schedule, fitting in a workout should be pretty easy because they are all very short in nature.

INTENSITY: WHAT EFFORT ARE YOU EXPECTED TO GIVE?

Simply, this is the amount of work you put in, in the time given. If you are given 30 seconds to perform an exercise, you need to be performing as many as you possible can fit in within the tie frame. If the exercise is not times, but rather repetitions. Each repetition needs to be 100% of your focus and effort.

The Warm Up

Warming your body up is essential. A comprehensive full- body workout will not only increase your body temperature, but also increase mobility, coordination and prepare your body for the workout ahead. Your brain will get fired up and your central nervous system will get prepped.

“

Never Skip Over Your WARM UP!

It is essential to remain healthy, prevent injuries and increase your performance.

FOAM ROLLING

The first part of your warm up is a self-myofascial release. This is the fancy term for a self-massage. This can be done with a foam roller, a hard ball such as a lacrosse ball or your own hands. You will apply pressure to specific parts of your body to remove knots, trigger points and scar tissue that accumulates in your body. By doing this self-massaging, you will eventually restore your muscles natural length and reduce lingering pains. This is a fairly quick process where you want to spend a few minutes rolling over your calves, quads, groin, hips, glutes, lats and upper back. Go over roughly 10 rolls on each of these parts, sticking on any particularly tight or tender spots. Once you are thoroughly rolled, you are onto the dynamic part of the warm up.

"
Before Anything Else, PREPARATION Is The Key To SUCCESS.
- Alexander Bell

Dynamic Warm Up

1.Jump Rope x 3mins

2.Big Arm Circles x 10 forward, 10 backwards

3.Front to Back Leg Swings x 10 each leg

4.Cross Body Leg Swings x 10 each leg

5.Lunges x 5 each leg

6.Squats with Arms Overhead x 10

7.Inch Worms x 5

8.Push-up x 10

9.Jumping Jacks x 25

10A. Jog Forward/ Jog Backwards x 15 yards

10B. Side Shuffle x 10 yards each way

10C. High Skips x 15 yards

"
It's Hard to Beat
A Person That
NEVER
GIVES UP!
-Babe Ruth

HERE IS THE GOOD STUFF.

REMEMBER TRAIN HARD, BUT SAFE!

1

BRUTAL BASICS

Prisoner Squats x 30 seconds

Push-ups x 30 seconds

Rest x 30seconds

REPEAT THIS PATTERN FOR A TOTAL OF 5 ROUNDS.

2

RACE TO 100 BURPEES

AS THE NAME IMPLIES, START A TIMER AND STOP IT ONCE YOU HAVE COMPLETED 100 FULL BURPEES.

3

PUSH-UP MADNESS

Wide Grip Push-ups x 12 reps

Push-ups x 9 reps

Diamond Push-ups x 6 reps

Clap Push-ups x 3 reps

REST FOR UP TO 2 MINUTES AND REPEAT FOR A TOTAL OF 3 TIMES.

4

AIR BORN INSANITY

Burpee x 2 reps

Jump Squat x 2 reps

Clap Push-up x 2 reps

COMPLETE AS MANY ROUNDS AS POSSIBLE IN 10 MINUTES.

5

ISOMETRIC KILLER

Wall Handstand x 30

seconds Plank x 30

seconds

Rest x 30 seconds

REPEAT THIS PATTERN FOR A TOTAL OF 5 ROUNDS.

6

POSTERIOR POWER

Glute Bridge x 10

Superman Raise x 10

Deep Squat x 10

REPEAT THIS CIRCUIT 4 TIMES WITH MINIMAL REST BETWEEN EACH.

“

Suffer The Pain Of DISCIPLINE, Or Suffer The Pain of REGRET.
- JIM ROHN

7

PULLING MADNESS

Inverted Row x 50 total reps

Chin-up x 40 total reps

Pull-up x 30 total reps

Dead Hang x 2 total minutes

REST AS NEEDED. JUST FINISH THE REPS PRESCRIBED ABOVE.

8

TRICEP TORTURE

Diamond Push-up x 30 seconds

Dips x 30 seconds

Bodyweight Tricep Extensions x 30 seconds

Rest 60 seconds

REPEAT THE PATTERN ABOVE FOR A TOTAL OF 5 ROUNDS.

9

SLOW STRENGTH PUSH-UPS

Each push-up will take 20 seconds to complete.

5 seconds hold at the top 5

seconds lowering

5 seconds at the bottom (1 inch from the floor)

5 seconds rising to the top.

COMPLETE AS MANY AS POSSIBLE
IN 10 MINUTES.

10

CRAWL SPRINT

Bear Crawl x 25 meters

Sprint Back x 25 meters

COMPLETE AS MANY ROUND AS POSSIBLE IN 15 MINUTES.

11

GASSERS

Set up cones at 10 meters, 20 meters, 30 meters, 40 meters and 50 meters.

Sprint to the first cone, then back to the start line.

Immediately sprint to the second cone and back to the start line.

Then to the third cone and back.

Forth cone and back.

Finally to the fifth cone and back.

THIS IS ONE GIANT SET. REST 2 MINUTES AND REPEAT 3 TIMES TOTAL.

12

BOXER STYLE

Burpees x 10 reps

Simulated Jump Rope x 100 reps

If you have access to a jump rope, perform 100 rope turns each round. If you do not have access to a rope, simulate the motion alternate foot hopping as if you were jumping rope.

COMPLETE 10 ROUNDS FOR A TOTAL OF 1000 ROPE TURNS AND 100 BURPEES.

13

JUMPING POWER

Box Jump x 2

Broad Jump x 4

Squat Jump x 8

Rest 60 seconds

REPEAT FOR A TOTAL OF 5 ROUNDS.

14

BASICS LADDER

Push-ups x 10,9,8,7,6,5,4,3,2,1

Squats x 10,9,8,7,6,5,4,3,2,1

Dips x 10,9,8,7,6,5,4,3,2,1

Pull-ups x 10,9,8,7,6,5,4,3,2,1

PERFORM THESE IN WHICH EVER ORDER YOU CHOOSE. IF YOU START WITH THE PULL-UPS FOR EXAMPLE YOU MUST COMPLETE ALL THE PRESCRIBED REPS BEFORE GOING ONTO THE NEXT EXERCISE.

15

CORE CRUSHER

Mountain Climber x 30 seconds

Plank x 30 seconds

Double Crunch x 30 seconds

Hollow Hold x 30 seconds

Rest 60 seconds

REPEAT FOR A TOTAL OF 3 TIMES

16

FEEL THE BURN!

Wall Squat x 30 seconds

Squat x 30 reps

REPEAT AS MANY TIMES AS POSSIBLE IN 10 MINUTES.

“

When You Are Going Through Hell KEEP GOING. - winston Churchill

17

DEATH BY BURPEE

Burpees x 1 rep, then 2 rep, then 3 rep up to 20 reps, then back down, 19 reps, 18 reps until you get back down to 1 again.

THIS IS A TOTAL OF 400 REPS.

18

FEEL LIKE A CLIMBER

Side to Side Pull-ups x 4 each

side Pull-up Hold x 10 seconds

REPEAT AS MANY TIMES AS POSSIBLE IN 15 MINUTES

19

HAND WALKS

Inch Worms x 5

Handstand Wall Walks x 3

REPEAT FOR A TOTAL OF 4 TIMES.

20

FIGHTERS FATIGUE

Shadow Box x 30 seconds

Sprawls x 30 seconds

Drop Steps x 30 seconds

Clinch Knees x 30 seconds

Shadow Box x 30 seconds

REPEAT FOR 8 ROUNDS TOTAL.

21

ANIMAL MADNESS

Bear Crawl x 20 seconds

Crab Walk x 20 seconds

Monkey Hops x 20 seconds

Rest 30 seconds

REPEAT FOR A TOTAL OF 10 ROUNDS

22

BURPEE SPRINTS

Sprint 20 meters

Burpee x 10 reps

REPEAT FOR 10 ROUNDS TOTAL

"
30 Minutes of
WORKOUT is Just
2% of Your Day.
NO EXCUSES

23

SPIDERMAN WORKOUT

Spiderman Push-up x 6 each side Spiderman Crawl x 10 meters Broad Jump x 5

REPEAT FOR A TOTAL OF 5 ROUNDS

24

SINGLES

Pistol Squat x 3 each leg

One arm push-up x 3 each arm

Complete the reps on the left side of your body before going onto the reps for the right side of your body.

COMPLETE FOR AS MANY ROUNDS AS POSSIBLE IN 10 MINUTES.

25

BIG 500

Squat x 100

Burpee x 100

Push-up x 100

Pull-up x 100

Dip x 100

NO GUIDELINES, REST AS YOU NEED, PERFORM AS YOU LIKE. JUST GET THE 500 REPS FINISHED.

26

AROUND THE WORLD

Bulgarian Spilt Squat x 30 seconds

Thai Push-ups x 30 seconds

Russian Twists x 30 seconds

Rest 30 seconds

REPEAT FOR A TOTAL OF 6 ROUNDS

27

NO CRUNCHES IN SIGHT

Flutter kicks x 50

Mountain Climber x 50

REST AS LITTLE AS POSSIBLE. REPEAT FOR A TOTAL OF 10 ROUNDS

28

BOXERS ENDURANCE

Jab Cross x 60 seconds

Alternating Uppercuts x 60 seconds

Alternating Hooks x 60 seconds

Rest 30 seconds

REPEAT FOR A TOTAL OF 5 ROUNDS

29

100 STEPS

Walking Lunges x 100 total reps per leg

Step ups at Mid Thigh Height x 100 total reps per leg

REST AS NEEDED, JUST COMPLETE ALL THE REPS PRESCRIBED.

30

HARDCORE 100

Burpee/Pull-up combo x 20

Clap Push-up x 20

Pistol Squat x 20 per leg

Tuck Jump x 20

COMPLETE THE REPS AS FAST AS POSSIBLE.

31

TABATA SPRINTS

Sprint Flat out for 10 seconds

Walk for 20 seconds

REPEAT THIS 10 TIMES.

32

200 REPS OF HELL

100 Judo Push-ups

100 Tuck Jumps

COMPLETE THE REPS HOWEVER YOU WANT, JUST GET THE REPS DONE.

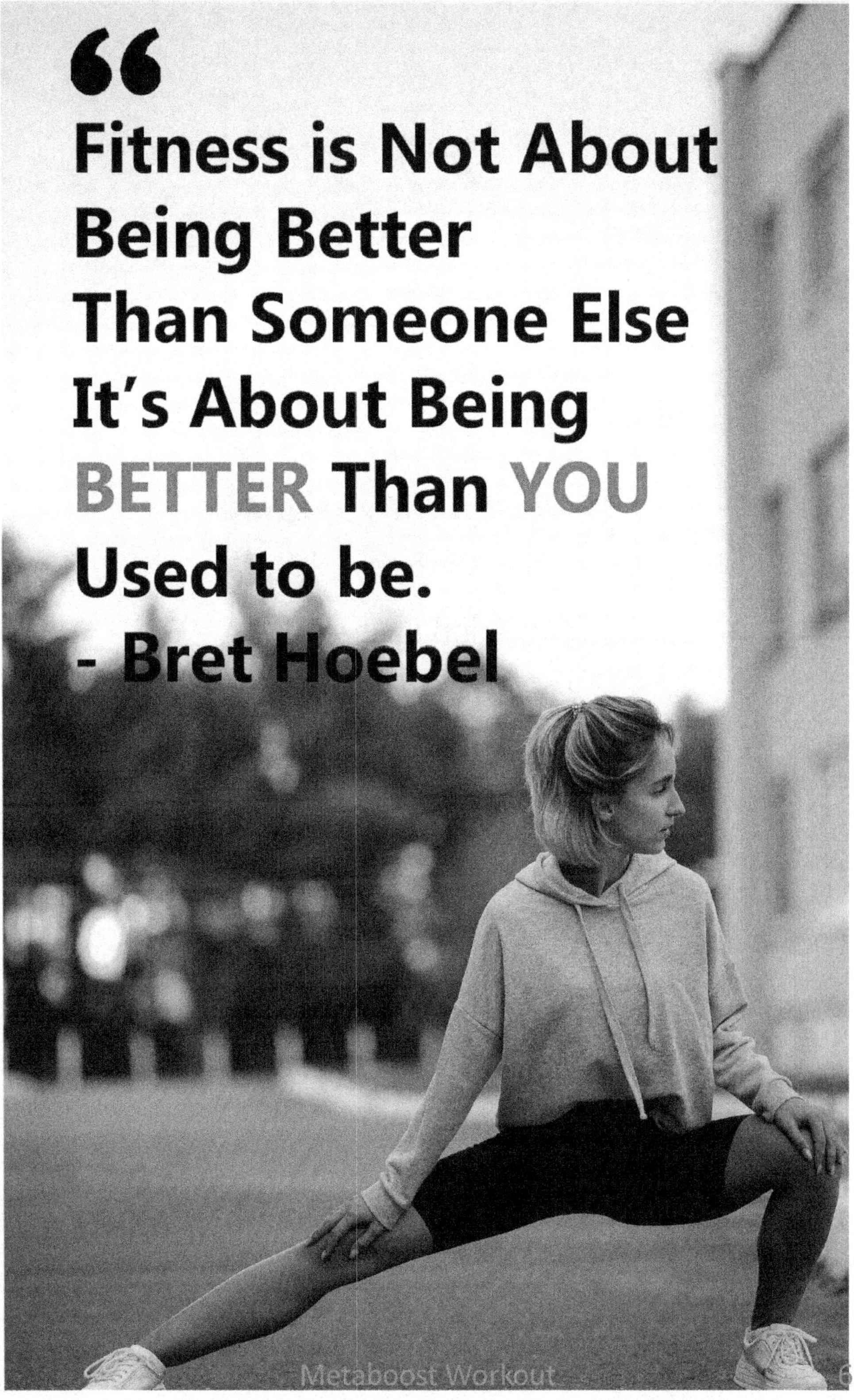
"
Fitness is Not About
Being Better
Than Someone Else
It's About Being
BETTER Than YOU
Used to be.
- Bret Hoebel

33

BOULDER SHOULDERS

Pike Push-up x 10

Handstand Push-up x 5

Handstand Hold x 30

seconds Rest 60 seconds

REPEAT 4 TIMES TOTAL.

34

BJJ ENDURANCE

Chin-up Holds x 20 seconds

Shrimp x 20 seconds

Technical Get-ups x 20 seconds

Egg Beaters x 20 seconds

Sit through x 20 seconds

Rest 30 seconds

REPEAT FOR A TOTAL OF 5 ROUNDS

35

ONE MOVE MURDER

BURPEE WITH PUSH-UP AND THE BOTTOM AND A TUCK JUMP AT THE TOP X AS MANY AS POSSIBLE IN 8 MINUTES.

36

LUNG BUSTER

Hill Sprint x 50 meters

Hindu Push-up x 10

COMPLETE 4 ROUNDS TOTAL.

37

LEGS DON'T STOP

Run 400 meters

Walk 100 meters

Run 300 meters

Walk 100 meters

Run 200 meters

Walk 100 meters

Run 100 meters

38

SPRINTERS DELIGHT

10 x 10 Meters Sprints- Rest 20 seconds between each. 5 x 100 Meters Sprints- Rest 60 seconds between each.

39

FINGER, HAND AND WRIST STRENGTH

Finger Push-ups x 5

Knuckle Push-ups x 10

Finger Push-up Hold x 10 seconds

Knuckle Push-up Hold x 20 seconds

COMPLETE 3 ROUNDS IN TOTAL, RESTING WELL BETWEEN EACH.

40

MORE ANIMAL MADNESS

Alligator Walk x 30 seconds

Duck Walk x 30 seconds

Kangaroo Hop x 30 seconds

Rest 30 seconds

REPEAT FOR A TOTAL OF 5 ROUNDS.

41

BEAR NECESSITIES

Bear Crawl for a total of 10 minutes.

DO THIS IS AS MANY SETS AS YOU WANT, RESTING WHENEVER YOU WANT. JUST GET A TOTAL TIME OF 10 MINUTES BEAR CRAWLING.

42

WALK, RUN, SPRINT

Walk x 60 seconds

Run x 60 seconds

Sprint x As long as possible.

CONTINUE THIS CYCLE UNTIL YOU HAVE COMPLETED 8 ROUNDS.

43

LATERAL THINKING

Lateral Step-ups x 10 each side

Lateral Lunges x 10 each side

Burpees with lateral Jump x 4 each side

Rest 60 seconds

REPEAT FOR A TOTAL OF 3 ROUNDS.

44

AS MANY AS POSSIBLE

Pull-ups x As many as you possibly can

Push-ups x As many as you possibly can

Squats x As many as you possibly can

"
MOTIVATION is What
Gets You Started.
HABIT is What
Keeps You
Going.
- Jim Ryan

45

FIGHTING AGAINST YOUR MIND

Wall Squat x failure

Inverted Row top position hold x failure

Back Bridge x failure

Plank x failure

Hollow Hold x failure

Push-up Bottom Position Hold x failure

Cliff Hanger x failure

REST WELL BETWEEN EACH EXERCISE AND BE SURE TO FIGHT AGAINST YOUR MIND TELLING YOU TO STOP. HOLD EACH FOR AS LONG AS PHYSICALLY POSSIBLE.

46

INVERTED WORLD

Hold a Handstand for a total time of 8 minutes.

47

99'S

Tuck Jumps x 33

Burpees x 33

Broad Jumps x 33

PERFORM THE REPS AS YOU LIKE, JUST COMPLETE THE REPS PRESCRIBED.

48

4 WAY CORE

Plank x 30 seconds

Left Side Plank x 30 seconds

Right Side Plank x 30 seconds

Superman Hold x 30 seconds

REPEAT FOR A TOTAL OF 3 TIMES.

49

LOAD OF L'S

L-sit Chin-up x 8 slow reps

L-sit Hold x failure

Hanging Leg Raise x 8 slow reps

THE KEY HERE IS PERFORMING THE REPS SLOW, INCREASING YOUR MUSCLES TIME UNDER TENSION. THIS CIRCUIT WILL ONLY NEED TO BE DONE 2 TIMES.

50

ROW AND GO

Inverted Rows x 12

Burpee x 12

PERFORM AS MANY ROUNDS AS POSSIBLE IN A 10 MINUTE PERIOD.

51

THE DIVE BOMBER

Complete a total of 250
Divebomber push-ups

52

MMA CONDITIONING

Jab Cross Sprawl x 60 seconds

Hip Escape/Shrimp x 60 seconds

Shadowbox x 60 seconds

Simulated Armbar from Mount x 60 seconds

Drop shots/Duckwalks x 60 seconds

Rest 60 seconds

CHALLENGERS COMPLETE 3 ROUNDS, CHAMPIONS COMPLETE 5 ROUNDS.

53

HOPPING MAD

Frog Jump x 100 meters

REST AS LONG AS YOU NEED AND COMPLETE 4 LENGTHS IN TOTAL.

54

RUN AGAINST THE CLOCK

On the minute Sprint 100 meters. Rest the remaining time left in the minute.

REPEAT THIS PATTERN UNTIL YOU CANNOT BEAT THE CLOCK ANYMORE.

55

EVEN MORE SADISTIC BURPEES

Begin flat on your back. Stand and perform a burpee with a push up at the bottom and a broad jump at the top.

COMPLETE AS MANY REPS AS POSSIBLE IN 5 MINUTES.

56

RUNNERS DELIGHT

Run as far as you can in 60 seconds

Walk for 60 seconds

REPEAT FOR A TOTAL OF 5 TIMES.

57

FIGHTERS 100

Straight Punches x

100 Clinch Knees x

100 Front Kicks x

100 Elbows x 100

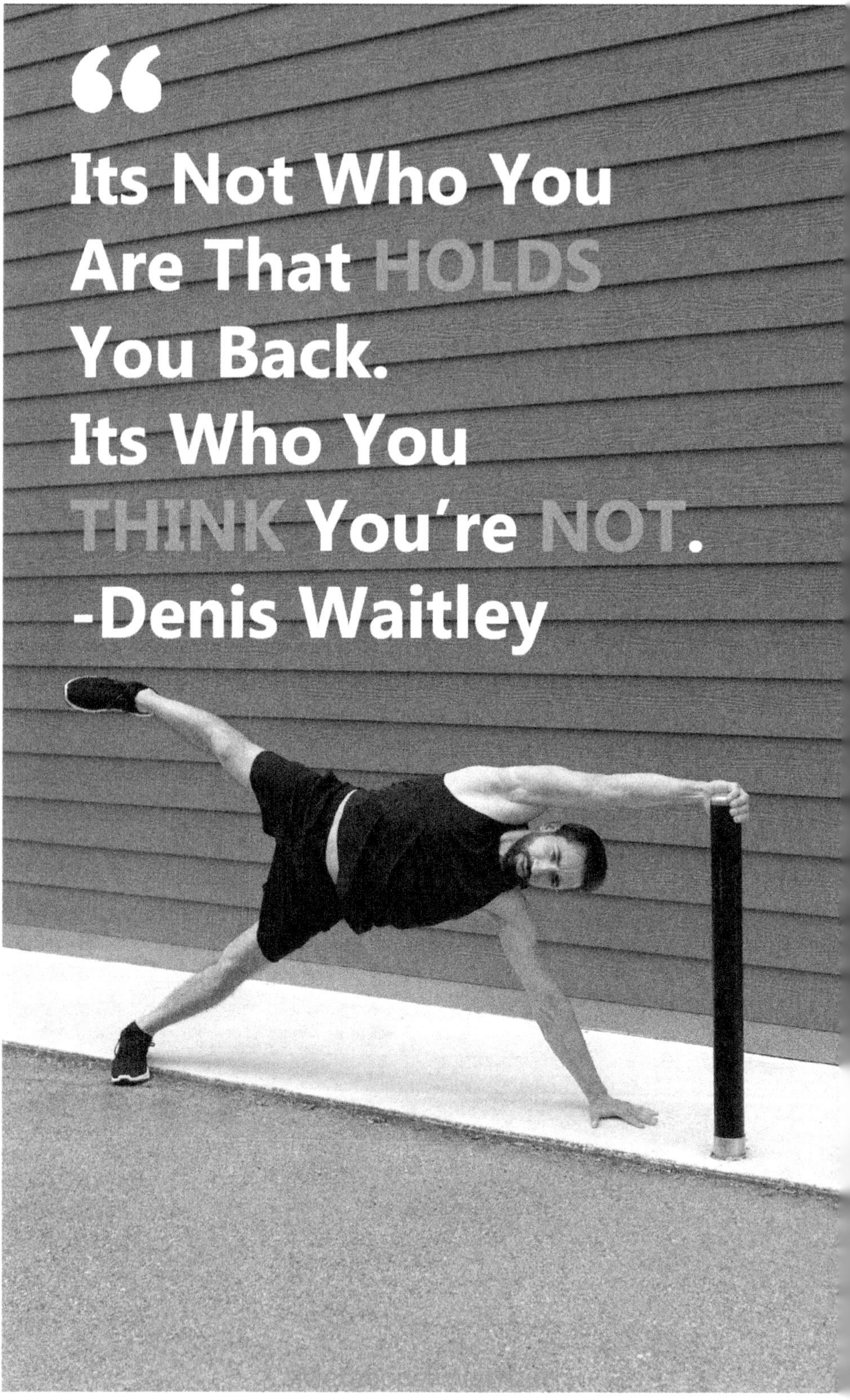
"
Its Not Who You
Are That HOLDS
You Back.
Its Who You
THINK You're NOT.
-Denis Waitley

58

TRADITIONAL TABATA

Flat out High Knee Sprint in place x 20 seconds

Light Shadowbox x 10 seconds

REPEAT THE PATTERN FOR A TOTAL OF 8 TIMES.

59

FEELING ON FIRE

Ab Bicycle x failure

Plank x failure

Mountain Climbers x failure

REST 60 SECONDS AND REPEAT FOR A TOTAL OF 5 TIMES.

60

DEFEND TO ATTACK

Sprawl to Jumping Knee x 100 total reps per leg

61

BYE BYE LEGS

Squats x 200

Burpee x 100

Tuck Jump x 75

Frog Jump x 50

Broad Jump x 25

PERFORM IN ANY ORDER YOU CHOOSE, JUST COMPLETE THE REPS PRESCRIBED.

62

GROUND FIGHTER COMPLEX

Sit Throughs x 20

per side Hindu

Push-ups x 20

COMPLETE AS MANY ROUNDS AS POSSIBLE IN 10 MINUTES.

63

THE ARCHER

Archer Push-ups x 5 each side

Archer Pull-ups x 3 each side

COMPLETE AS MANY ROUNDS AS POSSIBLE IN 15 MINUTES.

64

PISTOLEROS

Pistol Squats x
50 per leg

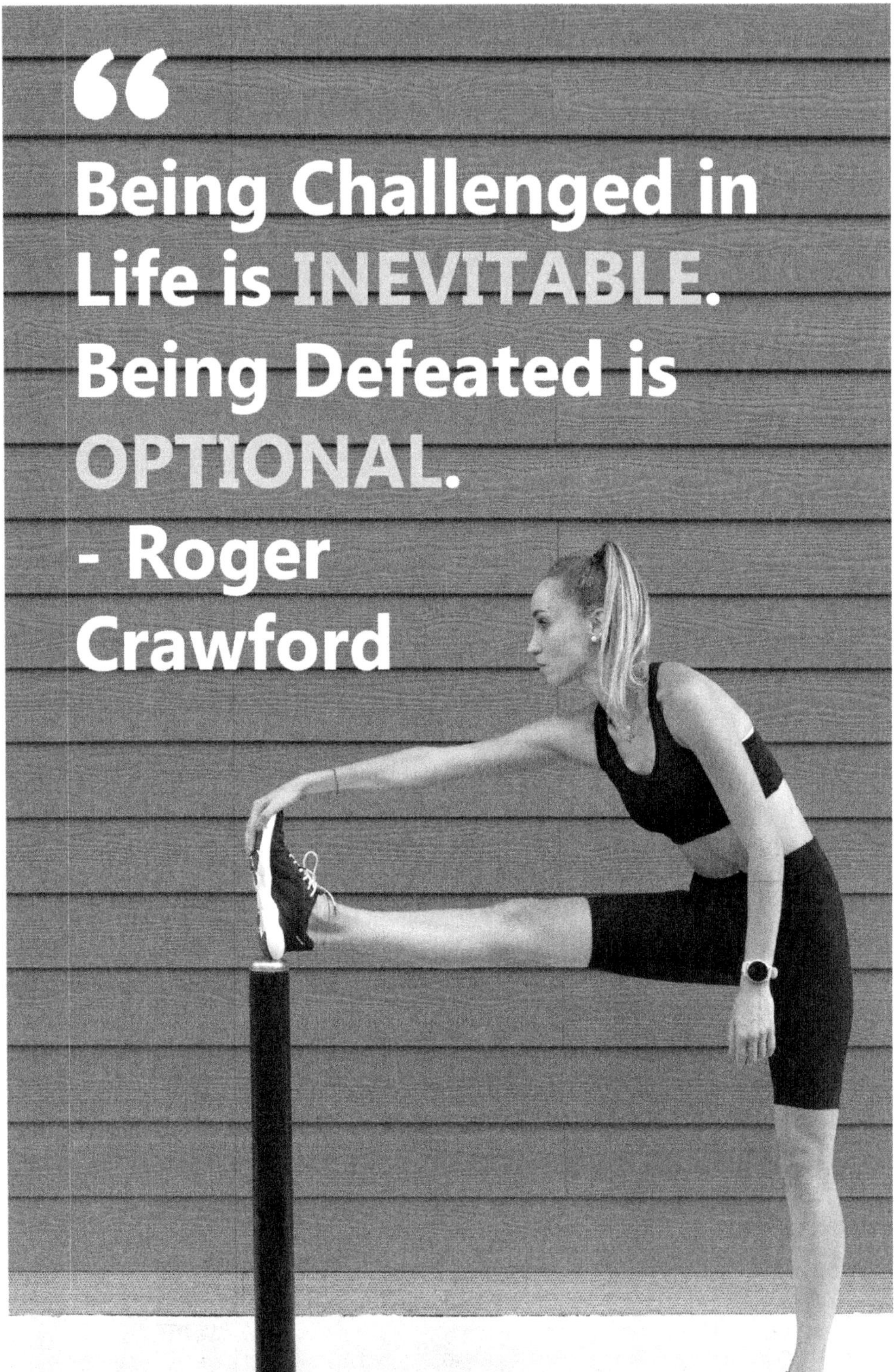
"
Being Challenged in Life is INEVITABLE.
Being Defeated is OPTIONAL.
- Roger Crawford

65

MONKEY FITNESS

Monkey Hops x 30 seconds

Chin-ups x 10

Monkey Hops x 30 seconds

Pull-ups x 5

Monkey Hops x 30 seconds

Dead Hang from bar x failure

REST AS NEEDED AND REPEAT FOR A TOTAL OF 3 TIMES.

66

FURIOUS BOX JUMPS

Burpee to Box Jump x 2

Box Jump x 4

Burpee x 6

Box Jump x 4

Burpee to Box Jump x 2

REST AS NEEDED, REPEAT FOR A TOTAL OF 3 TIMES.

67

HOLD AND EXPLODE

Wall Squat Hold x 30

seconds Squat Jump x 5

Push-up Bottom Hold x 30

seconds Clap Push-up x 5

Rest for 60 seconds

REPEAT THE CIRCUIT FOR A TOTAL OF 5 TIMES.

68

GYMNAST INSPIRED

Pseudo Planche Lean x 10 seconds

Handstand Hold x 20 seconds

Hollow Hold x 30 seconds

REST AS NEEDED AND REPEAT FOR A TOTAL OF 5 TIMES.

69

SLOWING TIME

Pull-up that takes a full 10 seconds to get to the bar Hold for 3 seconds at the bar

Take a further 10 seconds to lower to a Dead Hang Dead Hang for a further 3 seconds

COMPLETE 10 REPS TOTAL.

70

PUSH AND CRUNCH

Diamond Push-up x 10

Crunch x 40

Push-up x 20

Crunch x 30

Wide Grip Push-up x 30

Crunch x 20

REST 60 SECONDS AND REPEAT FOR A TOTAL OF 3 TIMES.

71

SINGLE LEG HELL

Cossack Squat x 50 total each leg Pistol Squats x 50 total each leg

72

ANCIENT MARTIAL ARTS

Horse Stance Hold x 10 Minutes Total

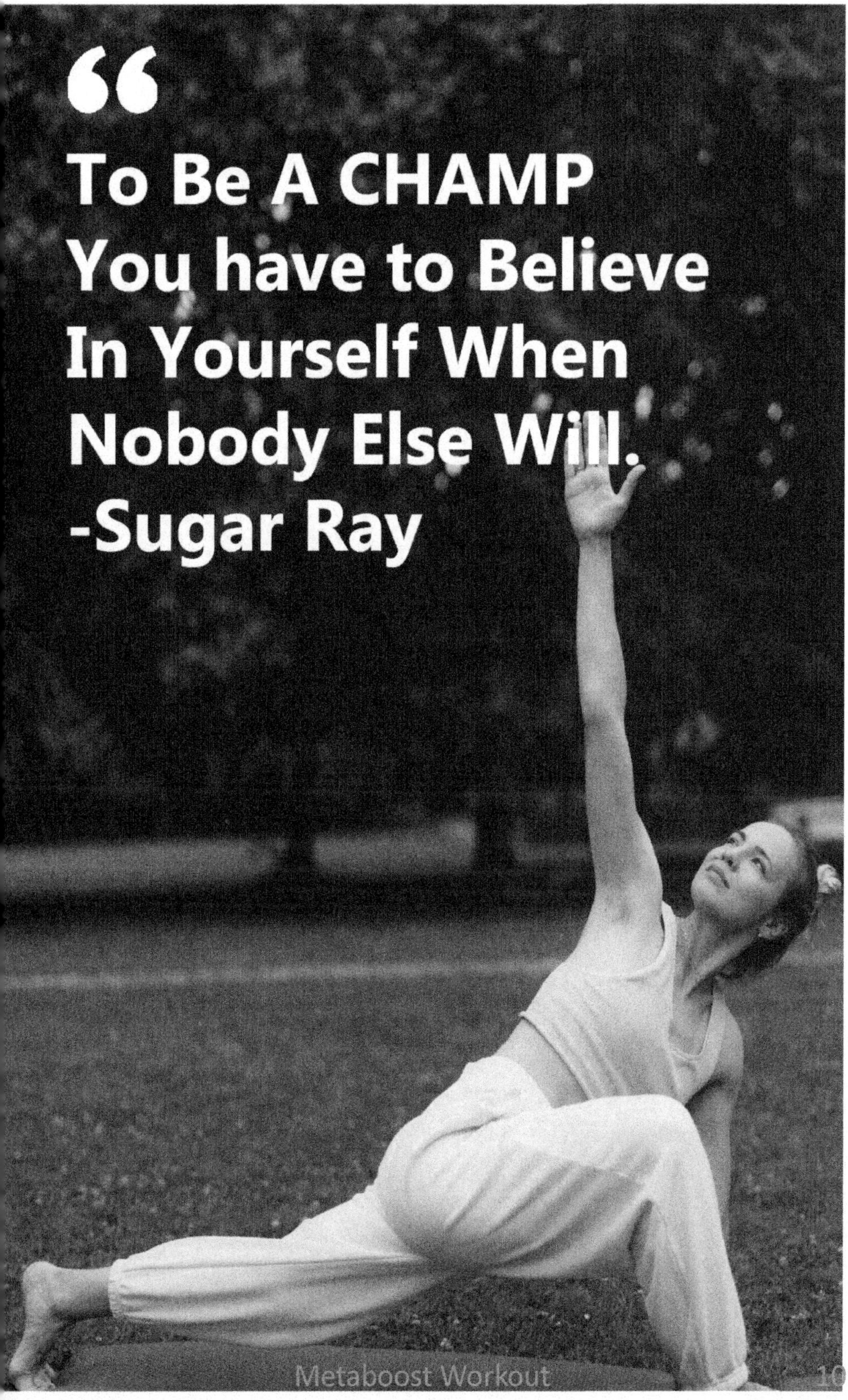
"
To Be A CHAMP
You have to Believe
In Yourself When
Nobody Else Will.
-Sugar Ray

73

SIMPLE BUT EFFECTIVE

Diamond Push-up x

10 Chin-up x 10

REST AS NEEDED, COMPLETE 10 ROUNDS IN TOTAL.

74

BANANA STYLE

Hollow Hold x 30 seconds

Superman Hold x 30 seconds

REST 30 SECONDS AND REPEAT FOR A TOTAL OF 4 ROUNDS.

75

DEAD MAN WALKING

Walking Lunge x 100 meters

REST 60 SECONDS AND REPEAT FOR A TOTAL OF 3 TIMES.

76

SUBMISSION SPECIAL

Kimura Sit-up x 10 each side

Guard Triangle attack x 10 each side

REPEAT FOR A TOTAL OF 5 ROUNDS.

77

HANDSTAND POWER

Handstand Hold x 30 seconds

Handstand Shoulder Taps x 10 each shoulder

78

PUSHING FROM ALL ANGLES

Handstand Push-up x 3

Pike Push-up x 6

Decline Push-up x 9

Push-up x 12

REST 90 SECONDS AND REPEAT FOR A TOTAL OF 3 ROUNDS.

79

TIGERS AND DRAGONS

Tiger Push-ups x 30 total

Dragon Flag x 30 total

80

HOP, SKIP, JUMP

Lateral Jumps x 30 seconds

Bounds x 30 seconds

Burpee x 30 seconds

REPEAT FOR A TOTAL OF 5 ROUNDS

81

HOW DOES SPIDERMAN DO IT?

Spiderman Crawl x 50 meters

Broad Jump x 50 meters

REST AS NEEDED, REPEAT FOR A TOTAL OF 3 TIMES.

"
The Meaning of
LIFE Is not Simply
To Exist. But To
Move AHEAD. TO
CONQUER.
- Arnold Schwarzenegger

82

HINDU STRENGTH

Hindu Squats x 250 total

Hindu Push-ups x 250 total

83

MENTAL TOUGHNESS TEST

400 meter run

50 Squats

300 meter run

50 Squats

200 meter run

50 Squats

100 meter run

50 Squats

84

TOWEL GRIP CIRCUIT

Towel Grip Pull-ups x

3 Towel Grip Chin-up

x 5 Towel Grip

Inverted Row x 7

Towel Isometric Squeeze x 10 seconds

REST 60 SECONDS AND REPEAT FOR A TOTAL OF 3 TIMES.

85

ISOMETRIC HELL

L-sit x failure

Tuck Planche x failure

Plank x failure

Right Side Plank x failure

Left Side Plank x failure

Bridge x failure

Hollow Hold x failure

PUSH YOURSELF ON EACH EXERCISE. YOU ARE ONLY PERFORMING EACH ONCE, SO MAKE IT COUNT!

86

ROCKY SPECIAL

Jump Rope Sprint x 100 rope turns

One Arm push-up x 3 each arm.

REPEAT FOR 5 TOTAL ROUNDS.

87

DIRTY 30

Dragon Flag x 10

Hanging Leg Raise x 10

Lying Leg Raise x 10

REST 90 SECONDS AND REPEAT FOR A TOTAL OF 3 TIMES.

88

FOOTBALL SPECIAL

Up Downs x 20 seconds

Lateral Shuffles x 20

seconds 10 Yard Sprint

REST 60 SECONDS AND REPEAT FOR A TOTAL OF 5 ROUNDS.

89

THE COMMANDO

Commando Pull-ups x 50
each side total.

90

GIANT ARMS CIRCUIT

Diamond Push-ups x 12

Bodyweight Tricep Extension x 10

Push-up x 10

Chin-up x 8

Bodyweight Bicep Curl x 6

REST 60 SECONDS AND REPEAT FOR A TOTAL OF 3 TIMES.

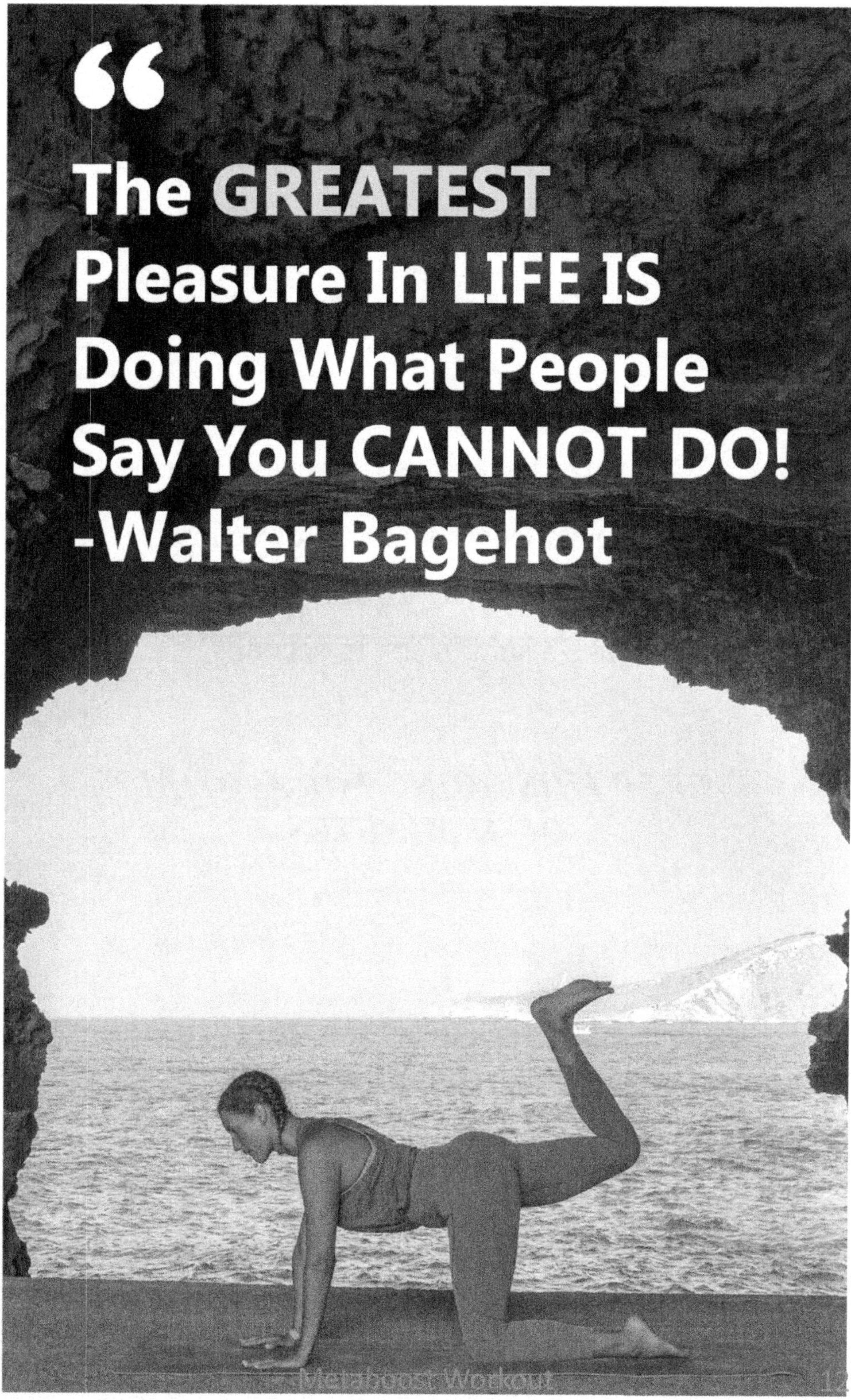
“
The GREATEST
Pleasure In LIFE IS
Doing What People
Say You CANNOT DO!
-Walter Bagehot

91

SHADOW WRESTLING

Stay in stance, move in all directions.

Sprawl ever 10 seconds.

Take a shot every 15 seconds

KEEP THIS GOING FOR A TOTAL OF 8 MINUTES.

92

HEART POUNDER

Burpee x 10 Squat x 1

Burpee x 9 Squat x 2

Burpee x 8 Squat x 3

Burpee x 7 Squat x 4

Burpee x 6 Squat x 5

Burpee x 5 Squat x 6

Burpee x 4 Squat x 7

Burpee x 3 Squat x 8

Burpee x 2 Squat x 9

Burpee x 1 Squat x 10

93

THE GRINDER

Push-ups x 2 minutes

Squats x 2 minutes

Pull-ups x 2 minutes

Burpee x 2minutes

94

HANGING GYMNAST

Skin the Cat x 3

Muscle-up x 1

REST AS MUCH AS NEEDED, REPEAT FOR A TOTAL OF 5 TIMES.

95

MUAY THAI ENDURANCE

Skipping Knee Twists x 30 seconds

Close Grip Chin-up x 30 seconds

Alternating Single Leg Knee

Bridge x 30 seconds

Spiderman Push-up x 30 seconds

Rest 30 seconds

REPEAT THE CIRCUIT FOR A TOTAL OF 6 TIMES.

96

TOTAL STRENGTH AND AGILITY

Alternating Pistol Squats x 100 total

Side to Side Push-ups x 100 total

Side to Side Pull-ups x 50 total

Handstand Hold x 5 minutes total

97

97 CORE HELL

Flutterkicks x 97 total

Plank Push-ups x 97

Mountain Climbers x 97 total

Hollow Hold x 97 seconds total

REST AS NEEDED. JUST GET THE REPS DONE.

98

POWER GLUTES

Glute Raises x 15

Deep Squat x 12

Reverse Plank x 60

seconds Rest 60 seconds

COMPLETE 5 ROUNDS TOTAL.

99

ADVANCED PUSH AND PULL

Handstand Push-up x

5 L-sit Pull-up x 5

Decline Push-up x 5

One Arm Inverted Row x 2 each arm

COMPLETE AS MANY ROUNDS AS POSSIBLE IN 15 MINUTES.

100

TOTAL STRENGTH AND AGILITY

Alternating Pistol Squats x 100 total

Side to Side Push-ups x 100 total

Side to Side Pull-up x 50 total

Handstand Hold x 5 minutes total

"
What DOESNT Kill You, Make You STRONGER.
-Nietzsche

THERE YOU HAVE IT, 100

WORKOUTS TO PUSH YOU TO NEW LEVELS OF FITNESS!

Frequently asked questions

WHEN SHOULD I USE THESE WORKOUTS?

The Metaboost Connection Program is designed for flexibility, making it perfect for busy individuals who want quick, effective results. These workouts are not meant to replace a full workout program but serve as a highly efficient resource for anyone short on time, aiming to improve cardiovascular health, and striving to shed fat quickly. Here's how you can incorporate these workouts:

•**Busy Days:** If you're pressed for time, use a Metaboost workout as your go-to session to keep your metabolism fired up.
•**Push Your Limits:** Use these high-intensity routines to challenge your cardio endurance and fat-burning potential.
•**Consistency is Key:** Stick to one workout per day, ensuring you give 100% effort and intensity every time. Even at just 15-20 minutes, these workouts pack a powerful punch when done with full dedication.

For athletes and coaches, these routines are excellent as **"finishers"** at the end of your training session.

Adding a Metaboost workout can maximize fat burn, build muscular endurance, and push your mindset to new levels—all while complementing the main part of your workout.

HOW SHOULD I USE THESE WORKOUTS?

The Metaboost Connection workouts are best used as a **guide** rather than a strict program. They are tailored for anyone looking for effective, equipment-free routines that can be completed in a short amount of time.

Follow these guidelines for optimal results:

1.Set Time Aside: Dedicate just 20-30 minutes to complete one of the workouts.
2.Stay Consistent: Aim to incorporate these sessions at least twice a week, and ideally, four times a week to see maximum benefits.
3.Scale to Your Fitness Level: Adjust the routines to match your current fitness abilities, but always maintain 100% effort and intensity.
4.Mix It Up: Choose a new workout each time to keep things challenging and prevent hitting a plateau. Avoid sticking to the same few routines—variety is key to progress.

These workouts are simple yet effective tools to help you stay on track, push your limits, and achieve your fitness goals with minimal time and equipment.

Whether you're a beginner or an experienced fitness enthusiast, the Metaboost Connection Program offers something for everyone.

HOW CAN I PUSH MYSELF AND BREAK THROUGH MY LIMITS?

The Metaboost Connection workouts are designed to help you unlock your full potential by challenging both your physical and mental limits.

For athletes and coaches, the competitive element is a powerful tool. Consider incorporating these routines as group challenges at the end of a training session. This added competition can motivate participants to push harder and reach new levels of fitness.

Even as you progress, it's inevitable that you'll revisit workouts you've already completed. Use this as an opportunity to measure your improvement. Track your time, reps, and how you felt the last time you completed the routine. Let these benchmarks motivate you to perform even better.

ARE THESE ROUTINES JUST FOR FAT LOSS?

Not at all! While fat loss is a common outcome of these workouts, the benefits go far beyond. These routines will help you:

•**Build Strength:** Gain lean muscle while becoming more athletic.

•**Improve Fitness:** Challenge your endurance, agility, and overall performance, regardless of your current fitness level.

•**Boost Athleticism:** Even seasoned athletes will find routines that test their limits and build new levels of strength and conditioning.

Whether your goal is to lose weight, build muscle, or enhance your athletic performance, the Metaboost Connection Program has you covered.

I'M STRUGGLING TO FIND THE MOTIVATION TO TRAIN. WHAT CAN I DO?

That's exactly why these workouts are here! The Metaboost routines are the ultimate excuse breakers.

•**Short Workouts, Big Impact:** Some of the routines take as little as 5 minutes, making them perfect for even the busiest schedules.

•**Fast and Effective:** You don't need hours to train—these high-intensity workouts deliver incredible results in minimal time.

•**Stay Accountable:** By prioritizing your health and carving out even small amounts of time, you'll begin to see results that motivate you to keep going.

Remember, getting fitter, leaner, and stronger starts with a choice. Make your health a priority, and the Metaboost Connection Program will guide you every step of the way.

These FAQs highlight how the Metaboost Connection Program isn't just a series of workouts—it's a mindset shift, a system to help you push through excuses, and a tool to help you achieve lasting results.

"

20 Years From Now,
You'll Be More
DISAPPOINTED
By The Things That
You Didn't Do.
Than By The Ones
You DID Do.
-Jackson Brown Jr.

About the Author

Charlie Shirk is a Colorado-based fitness coach redefining how people train by embracing the outdoors and unconventional tools like logs, rocks, and bodyweight exercises. His philosophy is simple: ***"Fitness isn't confined to a gym."***

Charlie's adaptive, no-nonsense approach helps clients build real-world strength and mental toughness. When he's not coaching, he shares his expertise through his blog, *Complete Fitness Connection,* offering tips on metabolic training, functional strength, and outdoor workouts.

Charlie's passion for breaking fitness norms continues to inspire people to embrace movement anywhere, anytime.

Printed in Great Britain
by Amazon

61450881R00087